THIS BOOK
BELONGS
TO

_____

DIFFICULT RIDDLES

1. I'm tall when I'm young and I'm short when I'm old. What am I?

2. Where can you find cities, towns, shops, and streets but no people?

3. There is a rooster sitting on top of a barn. If it laid an egg, which way would it roll?

4. What five letter word becomes shorter when you add two letters to it?

5. What is so fragile that saying its name breaks it?

6. What has a bottom at the top?

7. What has a face and two hands but no arms or legs?

8. How many months have 28 days?

9. What's black and white and read all over?

10. What word is spelled wrong in every dictionary?

11. I have no life, but I can die. What am I?

12. What gets wetter as it dries?

13. Mary has four daughters, and each of her daughters has a brother. How many children does Mary have?

14. You walk into a room which contains a match, a kerosene lamp, a candle, and a fireplace. What would you light first?

15. What has four wheels and flies?

16. What has 88 keys, but cannot open a single door?

17. What has a bed but never sleeps, can run but never walks, and has a bank but no money?

18. The more you take the more you leave behind. What are they?

19. What is full of holes but still holds water?

20. Who can shave 25 times a day but still have a beard?

21. What begins with T, finishes with T, and has "T" in it?

22. Which weighs more: a pound of feathers or a pound of bricks?

23. Everyone has it and no one can lose it; what is it?

24. What goes up but never goes back down?

25. What has one head, one foot, and four legs?

Fun Facts

A crocodile cannot stick its
tongue out

A shrimp's heart is in its head

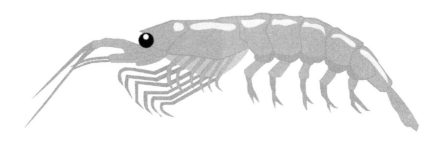

26. What begins with an E but only has one letter in it?

27. I am an odd number. Take away a letter and I become even. What number am I?

28. After a train crashed, every single person died. Who survived?

29. What gets bigger the more you take away?

30. Three men were in a boat. It capsized, but only two got their hair wet. Why?

31. I'm always on the dinner table, but you don't get to eat me. What am I?

32. David's father has three sons: Snap, Crackle, and _____?

33. What belongs to you, but other people use it more than you?

34. What is more useful when it is broken?

35. I make two people out of one. What am I?

36. I am white when I am dirty, and black when I am clean. What am I?

37. They have not flesh, nor feathers, nor scales, nor bone. Yet they have fingers and thumbs of their own. What are they?

38. This is as light as a feather, yet no man can hold it for long. What am I?

39. How do you spell COW in thirteen letters?

40. Before Mount Everest was discovered, what was the highest mountain on Earth?

41. The more you take away, the more I become. What am I?

42. I am the beginning of the end, and the end of time and space. I am essential to creation, and I surround every place. What am I?

43. What goes up when the rain comes down?

44. What did the baseball glove say to the ball?

45. I have no feet, no hands, no wings, but I climb to the sky. What am I?

46. If you have me, you want to share me. If you share me, you haven't got me. What am I?

47. What are moving left to right, right now?

48. There is an ancient invention, still used in some parts of the world today, that allows people to see through walls. What is it?

49. What did the bee say to the flower?

50. If you were running a race, and you passed the person in 2nd place, what place would you be in now?

Fun Facts

Like fingerprints, everyone's tongue print is different

A shark is the only fish that can blink with both eyes

51. I have a heart that never beats, I have a home, but I never sleep. I can take a man's house and build another's, and I love to play games with my many brothers. I am a king among fools. Who am I?

52. I have a thousand needles, but I do not sew. What am I?

53. How many times can you subtract the number 5 from 25?

54. Sometimes I am born in silence, Other times, no. I am unseen, But I make my presence known. In time, I fade without a trace. I harm no one, but I am unpopular with all. What am I?

55. I reach for the sky, but clutch to the ground; sometimes I leave, but I am always around. What am I?

56. What question can someone ask all day long, always get completely different answers, and yet all the answers could be correct?

57. Which one of Santa's reindeer can you see in outer space?

58. What can you hold in your right hand, but not in your left?

59. What asks no questions but requires many answers?

60. I run in and out of town all day and night. What am I?

61. Why can't a pirate ever finish the alphabet?

62. What do you call a bear with no teeth?

63. A slender body, a tiny eye, no matter what happens, I never cry. What am I?

64. What two things can you never eat for breakfast?

65. What is the end of everything?

66. There is a clerk at the butcher shop, he is five feet ten inches tall, and he wears size 13 sneakers. He has a wife and 2 kids. What does he weigh?

67. Why is Peter Pan always flying?

68. If 5 cats catch 5 mice in 5 minutes, how long will it take one cat to catch a mouse?

69. What is faster hot or cold?

70. What is the longest word in the dictionary?

71. What four-legged animal can jump higher than a house?

72. I pass before the sun yet make no shadow. What am I?

73. What is the hardest key to turn?

74. What jack has a head but no body?

75. What question can never be answered with a Yes?

76. How many of each type of animal did Moses take on the Ark?

77. What relation would your father's sister's sister-in-law be to you?

78. Which one of Santa's reindeer is the fastest?

79. Why are Christmas trees bad at knitting?

Fun Facts

Tigers have striped skin, not just striped fur

The giant squid has the largest eyes in the world

80. What did the triangle say to the circle?

81. No matter how smart you are, there is one thing you will always overlook. What is it?

82. Why did the outlaw steal the deck of cards?

83. A boy fell off of a 100-foot ladder, but he did not get hurt. How is this possible?

84. What is bigger than a grey elephant yet weighs nothing. What is it?

85. What kind of music can you hear in space?

86. When I point up it is bright, but when I point down it's dark. What am I?

87. How do spiders communicate?

88. What do you call a person who is afraid of Santa Claus?

89. When was the latest year that is the same upside down?

90. Where do you take a sick pirate ship?

91. What can be picked but not chosen?

92. I have four legs but never walk I may be covered in flowers but have no soil I hold food three times a day but never eat a meal. What am I?

93. Why are teddy bears never hungry?

94. I am served at a table, in gatherings of two or four; Served small, white, and round. You will love some, And that's part of the fun. What am I?

95. Pick a number from 1-10, multiply it by 2, add ten, divide it by 2, now subtract the number that you have from the number you picked. What is it?

96. What do you call a fish with no eye's?

97. How many bricks does it take to complete a brick building?

98. There is a bus full of people travelling over San Francisco and no one gets off the bus throughout the journey. But when it gets to the other side there is not a single person left. How is this possible?

99. Saws sing it, we snore it, Bees drone it; And one alone ends the alphabet. What is it?

100. If fish lived on land, where would they live?

FUN FACTS

The Queen has two birthdays

There are more stars in space than there are grains of sand on a beach

FIENDISH RIDDLES

101. What is put on a table, cut, but never eaten?

102. What colour is the wind?

103. What tastes better than it smells?

104. What falls often but never gets hurt?

105. Why should you never iron a 4-leaf clover?

106. If a dog is tied to a piece of rope that is 6m long, how can he reach a bone that is 7m away?

107. You're sitting down for breakfast and realize you have 4 bagels left. You know you will run out in four

days, so you cut them in half. How many bagels do you have now?

108. When it is alive we sing, when it is dead we clap our hands. What is it?

109. What is in seasons, seconds, centuries, and minutes but not in decades, years or days?

110. I'm always in charge, I'm never in debt. I'm known as the first amongst all my kind. I'm found within cars, but never in buses. I'm not used in Mexico; I'm used in Palestine. What am I?

111. As I was going to the fair, I saw a man with golden hair. He had 3 sons each with another one. How many people were going to the fair?

112. Sally has four classes, Science, Math, English Language Arts, and History. She had a test in every class, and wanted to have some fun, so she did all her tests in French. When she received her tests back, only

one teacher could understand her work. If none of Sally's teachers spoke French, which teacher was able to understand the test and how did they understand it?

113. What U.S. state makes the most writing utensils?

114. When liquid splashes me, none seeps through. When I am moved a lot, liquid I spew. When I am hit, colour I change. And colour, I come in quite a range. What I cover is very complex, and I am very easy to flex. What am I?

115. I'm flat when I'm new. I'm fat when you use me. I release my gas when something sharp touches me. What am I?

116. It doesn't bark, it doesn't bite but it still won't let you in the house. What is it?

117. I saw a man in white, he looked quite a sight. He was not old, but he stood in the cold. And when he felt

the sun, he started to run. Please answer me. Who could he be?

118. Three men are walking across a green and luscious field. Only two of them are wearing rubber boots and yet the feet of the third man remain dry. Why?

119. Something that requires our mental skill to decode it, our imagination to understand it, our knowledge is tested to its max, it confuses us at every stage, it seems easy yet difficult, only those who are used to, will get through. What is it?

120. A hundred feet in the air, but it's back is on the ground. What is it?

121. What happens to a small stone that works up its courage?

Fun Facts

Horses and cows sleep standing up

It would take only an hour to drive to space

122. I lead the way into the unknown and bring strength where there is fear. I am the creator of invention, and the maker of all adventure. What am I?

123. Even if they are starving, natives living in the Arctic will never eat a penguin's egg. Why not?

124. I sleep by day; I fly by night. I have no feathers to aid my flight. What am I?

125. A mother had five boys Marco, Tucker, Webster and Thomas. Was the fifth boys name Frank, Evan or Alex?

126. What familiar word starts with IS, ends with AND, and has LA in the middle?

127. I am a riddle that the answer is gone. Get it right, you have until dawn. What is it?

128. What did one wall say to the other wall?

129. I speak without a mouth and hear without ears. I have no body, but I come alive with the wind. What am I?

130. Even if you give this to someone else, you still get to keep it. What is it?

131. How do you divide the sea in half?

132. Which one of Santa's reindeer do you see at a competition?

133. Where is the AD before BC, tomorrow before yesterday, and the eight is first?

134. Remove my fourth letter and the first three letters will spell a school subject. My last five letters spell something that happens when swallowing a carrot whole. My whole spells a vegetable. What am I?

135. Your mom has 4 kids, one named North, another called South, and East. What is the last child's name?

136. I am a five-letter word and I am a fruit. Take out the first and second letter and I am an animal, take out the first and last letter and I am a type of music. What am I?

137. You must keep this thing; its loss will affect your brothers. For once yours is lost, it will soon be lost by others. What is it?

138. What kind of a band, never plays music?

139. There were two pairs hanging on a tree, one man walked by and took a pair. Soon after a second man also took a pear from the tree. However, even after both

men took fruit from the tree there was still a pear left on the tree. How could this be?

140. How do you make "one" disappear?

141. If you have 10 peaches and take 7 peaches away, how many do you have?

142. Why did the man stare at the can of orange juice?

143. What word doesn't belong in this group? That, hat, what, mat, cat, sat, pat, or chat?

144. Why did the radish turn red?

145. What is it that smells most in a perfume shop?

146. What kind of tree can you carry in your hand?

Fun Facts

Water covers 70% of the earth

Kangaroos can't walk backwards

147. Which word is the odd one out: First, Second, Third, Forth, Fifth, Sixth, Seventh, and Eighth?

148. What do you serve that you cannot eat?

149. This object can be driven, but has no wheels, and can also be sliced and remain whole. What is it?

150. What do you throw out to use and take in when you're done?

151. What has 18 legs and catches flies?

152. What animal always goes to bed with shoes on?

153. Seven kids are in line for a carnival ride. Third in line is Joe, and two spots ahead of him is Kylie. Seventh in line is Kate, in front of Kate is Rylie, behind Joe is Chris, Elizabeth is ahead of John in line. What is the order of the line?

154. If it takes 3 people to dig I hole how many people does it takes for 1/2 a hole?

155. What lives in winter, dies in summer, and grows with its roots upward?

156. How do you make a strawberry shake?

157. What is something you don't own but you can give it to anyone you meet? You only have one, but you can give it away as many times as you want without losing it. What is it?

158. Tear off one and scratch its head, what was red is now black instead. What is It?

159. The pet shop starts with some dogs, then someone comes and takes I of the dogs, then another person and their child take 4 dogs. After that a mother, father and their 18 kids adopt 12 dogs. Then the pet

shop receives 3 dogs, and someone takes 1, now the pet shop has 2 dogs. How many dogs did they have at the beginning?

160. Why did the man hold a shoe to his ear?

161. What chins are never shaved?

162. Three matches are sitting on a table. Without adding another make for three matches four. You are not allowed to break any of the matches.

163. What islands should have good singers?

164. What has teeth that is kept in the house, but is never used for eating?

165. What does a rain cloud wear under their raincoat?

166. What country would you send a man to for his appetite?

167. Through me you see through things. What am I?

168. Look in my face, I am somebody; Look in my back, I am nobody. What am I?

169. How can you leave a room with two legs and return with six legs?

170. Why was the broom late?

171. Why do mummies like Christmas so much?

172. What kind of goose fights with snakes?

Fun Facts

About 70% of an adult's body is made of water

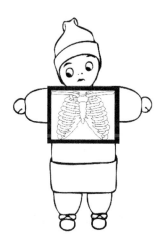

You cannot talk and inhale or exhale at the same time... try it!

173. I run all around the pasture but never move. What am I?

174. I act like a cat, I look like a cat, Yet I am not a cat. What am I?

175. What food lives at the beach?

176. You have 5 kids and you must get them all into a car. Tommy and Timmy are twins, but they fight so they can't sit together. Sarah and Sally fight too, so they can't sit together. Max fights with his sisters so he can only sit by his brothers. There's 5 seats side by side and you have to put them in order. How would you seat the kids, so that everyone is happy?

177. Why does the teacher wear sunglasses when she comes to the class?

178. What has toes but no feet or legs?

179. There is a clerk at the butcher shop, he is five feet ten inches tall, and he wears size 13 sneakers. He has a wife and 2 kids. What does he weigh?

180. A murderer is condemned to death. He has to choose between three rooms. The first is full of raging fires, the second is full of assassins with loaded guns, and the third is full of lions that haven't eaten in 3 years. Which room is safest for him?

181. A farmer has twenty sheep, ten pigs and ten cows. If we call the pigs cows, how many cows will he have?

182. Why did the kid bring a ladder to school?

183. How many seconds are there in one year?

184. Why did Tigger go to the bathroom?

185. There was a green house. Inside the green house there was a white house Inside the white house there

was a red house. Inside the red house there were lots of babies. What am I?

186. What time does a tennis player get up?

187. A man in a car saw a golden door, silver door, and a bronze door. What door did he open first?

188. Some months have 30 days; some months have 31 days. How many have 28?

189. How do vampires like their food served?

190. The more there is the less you see. What is it?

191. What goes up and down stairs without moving?

192. Why was six afraid of seven?

193. What's brown and sticky?

194. What do ghosts eat on Halloween?

195. What type of cheese is made backwards?

196. How do you get straight A's?

197. I went into the woods and got it, I sat down to seek it, I brought it home with me because I couldn't find it.

198. What animal keeps the best time?

199. Which case is not a case?

200. What do you get from a pampered cow?

Fun Facts

Your heart is about the same
size as your fist

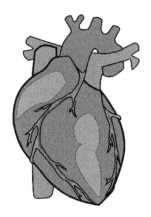 

Frogs drink water through their
skin

IMPOSSIBLE RIDDLES

201. Why don't dogs make good dancers?

202. You can see me in water, but I never get wet. What am I?

203. What is always in front of you, but can't be seen?

204. There's a one-story house in which everything is yellow. Yellow walls, yellow doors, yellow furniture. What colour are the stairs?

205. What can you break, even if you never pick it up or touch it?

206. A man dies of old age on his 25th birthday. How is this possible?

207. I have branches, but no fruit, trunk, or leaves. What am I?

208. I'm found in socks, scarves and mittens; and often in the paws of playful kittens. What am I?

209. What can't be put in a saucepan?

210. What has lots of eyes, but can't see?

211. What can you catch, but not throw?

212. What can travel all around the world without leaving its corner?

213. What has a head and a tail but no body?

214. What building has the most stories?

215. What kind of coat is best put on wet?

216. If two's company, and three's a crowd, what are four and five?

217. What three numbers, none of which is zero, give the same result whether they're added or multiplied?

218. Three doctors said that Bill was their brother. Bill says he has no brothers. How many brothers does Bill actually have?

219. Two fathers and two sons are in a car, yet there are only three people in the car. How?

220. The day before yesterday I was 21, and next year I will be 24. When is my birthday?

221. A little girl goes to the store and buys one dozen eggs. As she is going home, all but three break. How many eggs are left unbroken?

222. A man describes his daughters, saying, "They are all blonde, but two; all brunette but two; and all redheaded but two." How many daughters does he have?

223. A girl has as many brothers as sisters, but each brother has only half as many brothers as sisters. How many brothers and sisters are there in the family?

224. A word I know, six letters it contains, remove one letter and 12 remains. What is it?

225. What would you find in the middle of Toronto?

226. Two in a corner, one in a room, zero in a house, but one in a shelter. What is it?

Fun Facts

A pet hamster can run up to 8
miles per night

Monkeys can go bald with old
age just like humans

227. What 4-letter word can be written forward, backward or upside down, and can still be read from left to right?

228. Forward I am heavy, but backward I am not. What am I?

229. What is 3/7 chicken, 2/3 cat and 2/4 goat?

230. I am a word of letters three; add two and fewer there will be. What word am I?

231. What word of five letters has one left when two are removed?

232. What word is pronounced the same if you take away four of its five letters?

233. I am a word that begins with the letter "I." If you add the letter "a" to me, I become a new word with a

different meaning, but that sounds exactly the same. What word am I?

234. What word in the English language does the following: The first two letters signify a male, the first three letters signify a female, the first four letters signify a great, while the entire world signifies a great woman. What is the word?

235. A man calls his dog from the opposite side of the river. The dog crosses the river without getting wet, and without using a bridge or boat. How?

236. What can fill a room but takes up no space?

237. I turn once, what is out will not get in. I turn again, what is in will not get out. What am I?

238. People make me, save me, change me, raise me. What am I?

239. What breaks yet never falls, and what falls yet never breaks?

240. I am always hungry and will die if not fed, but whatever I touch will soon turn red. What am I?

241. The person who makes it has no need of it; the person who buys it has no use for it. The person who uses it can neither see nor feel it. What is it?

242. A man looks at a painting in a museum and says, "brothers and sisters I have none, but that man's father is my father's son." Who is in the painting?

243. With pointed fangs I sit and wait; with piercing force I crunch out fate; grabbing victims, proclaiming might; physically joining with a single bite. What am I?

244. When you look for something, why is it always in the last place you look?

245. A cowboy rode into town on Friday. He stayed in town for three days and rode out on Friday. How was that possible?

246. How can a man go 8 days without sleep?

247. Can you name three consecutive days without using the words Wednesday, Friday, and Sunday?

248. What has three feet but cannot walk?

249. What gets sharper the more you use it?

250. They come out at night without being called and are lost in the day without being stolen. What are they?

251. Two in front, two in behind, and one in the middle. How many are there?

Fun Facts

One of the ingredients needed to make dynamite is peanuts

Hippopotamus milk is pink

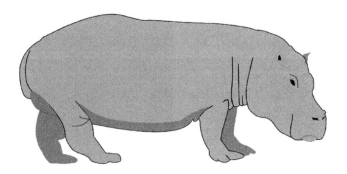

252. What is easy to get into, but hard to get out of?

253. What word contains 26 letters, but only three syllables?

254. What has a neck but no head?

255. A bat and a ball cost $1.10. The bat costs $1.00 more than the ball. How much does the ball cost?

256. I have no eyes, no ears, and legs, and yet I help move the earth. What am I?

257. First, I threw away the outside and cooked the inside. Then I ate the outside and threw away the inside. What did I eat?

258. What has words but never speaks?

259. Why are ghosts such bad liars?

260. What tire doesn't move when the car turns right?

261. What do you call a sad strawberry?

262. Why couldn't the moon finish his meal?

263. What room doesn't have any windows?

264. What do you call a grandfather clock?

265. What goes up and down the stairs without moving?

266. Where do fish keep their money?

267. Why can't you give Elsa a balloon?

268. If the red house is on the right and the blue house is on the left, where is the white house?

269. What 8 letter word can have a letter taken away and it still makes a word. Take another letter away and it still makes a word. Keep on doing that until you have one letter left. What is the word?

270. What has a head, a tail, is brown, and has no legs?

271. A doctor and a bus driver are both in love with the same woman, an attractive girl named Sarah. The bus driver had to go on a long bus trip that would last a week. Before he left, he gave Sarah seven apples. Why?

272. What room do ghosts avoid?

273. You live in a one-story house made entirely of redwood. What colour would the stairs be?

274. Re-arrange the letters, O O U S W T D N E J R, to spell just one word. What is it?

275. Mr. and Mrs. Mustard have six daughters and each daughter has one brother. How many people are in the Mustard family?

276. What has six faces, but does not wear makeup, has twenty-one eyes, but cannot see? What is it?

277. A woman shoots her husband. Then she holds him underwater for over 5 minutes. Finally, she hangs him. But 5 minutes later they both go out together and enjoy a wonderful dinner together. How can this be?

278. Why is Europe like a frying pan?

Fun Facts

The average person spends 2 weeks of their life waiting at traffic lights

Cans of diet soda will float in water, regular soda cans will sink

279. What can point in every direction but can't reach the destination by itself.

280. Two fathers and two sons went fishing one day. They were there the whole day and only caught 3 fish. One father said, that is enough for all of us, we will have one each. How can this be possible?

281. I am taken from a mine, and shut up in a wooden case, from which I am never released, and yet I am used by almost everybody. What am I?

282. There are two monkeys on a tree, and one jumps off. Why does the other monkey jump too?

283. Lovely and round, I shine with pale light, grown in the darkness, A lady's delight. What am I?

284. What can be stolen, mistaken, or altered, yet never leaves you your entire life?

285. I have a big mouth and I am also quite loud! I am NOT a gossip, but I do get involved with everyone's dirty business. What am I?

286. Until I am measured, I am not known. Yet how you miss me when I have flown. What am I?

287. I have four wings, but cannot fly, I never laugh and never cry; On the same spot I'm always found, toiling away with little sound. What am I?

288. I weaken all men for hours each day. I show you strange visions while you are away. I take you by night, by day take you back, none suffer to have me, but do from my lack. What am I?

289. He has married many women but has never been married. Who is he?

290. What do you throw out when you want to use it but take in when you don't want to use it?

291. What has no hands but might knock on your door, and if it does you better open up?

292. Often held but never touched, always wet but never rusts, often bites but seldom bit, to use me well you must have wit. What am I?

293. When you buy me I am costly, but the only use I have is just hanging. What am I?

294. Rock and roll, rock and roll. What rocks but does not roll?

295. What is both possible and impossible at the same time?

296. Two men were playing tennis. They played five sets and each man won three sets. How can this be possible?

297. Why did the squirrel lay only its back on the river?

298. A prisoner is told "If you tell a lie we will hang you; if you tell the truth we will shoot you." What can he say to save himself?

299. Which three letters can frighten a thief away?

300. What fastens two people yet touches only one?

Fun Facts

On the planet Venus it rains metal

If a donkey and a zebra have a baby, it is called a zonkey

ANSWERS

DIFFICULT RIDDLES

1. A candle

2. A map

3. Roosters don't lay eggs

4. Short (short+er)

5. Silence

6. Your legs

7. A clock

8. All twelve of them do

9. A newspaper

10. Wrong

11. A battery

12. A towel

13. Five. Each daughter has the same single brother.

14. The match

15. A garbage truck

16. A piano

17. A river

18. Footsteps

19. A sponge

20. A barber

21. A teapot

22. They weigh the same

23. A shadow

24. Your age

25. A bed

26. An envelope

27. Seven

28. All of the couples

29. A hole

30. One was bald

31. Plates and silverware

32. David

33. Your name

34. An egg

35. A mirror

36. A blackboard

37. Gloves

38. Your breath

39. SEE O DOUBLE YOU

40. Mount Everest

41. A hole

42. The letter e. End, timE, spacE, Every place

43. An umbrella

44. Catch you later

45. Smoke

46. A secret

47. Your eyes

48. A window

49. Hello honey

50. You would be in the 2nd place. You thought first place, right? Well, you passed the guy in second place, not first.

51. The King of Hearts in a deck of cards

52. A porcupine

53. Once, because after you subtract it's not 25 anymore

54. A fart

55. A tree

56. 'What time is it?'

57. Comet

58. Your left hand

59. A doorbell

60. A road

61. Because they always get lost at sea

62. A gummy bear

63. A needle

64. Lunch and dinner

65. The letter 'g'

66. Meat

67. He Neverlands

68. Five minutes

69. Hot, you can easily catch a cold

70. Smiles (there is a mile between the two S's)

71. Any, Houses can't jump

72. The wind

73. A don-key

74. Jack-o-lantern

75. 'Are you asleep?'

76. None, it was Noah

77. This person would be your mother

78. Dasher

79. Because they always drop their needles

80. 'You're pointless'

81. Your nose

82. He heard there were 13 diamonds in it

83. He was only on the first step

84. The elephants shadow

85. A nep-tune

86. A light switch

87. Through the worldwide web

88. Claustraophobic

89. 1961

90. To the dock

91. A nose

92. A table

93. Because they are stuffed

94. Ping pong balls

95. Do you have 5?

96. Fsh

97. One brick

98. They are all married

99. Zzzzzzz

100. In Finland

FIENDISH RIDDLES

101. Cards

102. Blew

103. A tongue

104. Snow

105. You don't want to press your luck

106. The other end is not tied to anything

107. 4 Bagels

108. Birthday candle

109. The letter 'n'

110. The letter 'a'

111. One. Just me because I met the others on the way to the fair

112. The Math teacher, because numbers are the same in French as they are in English

113. Pencil-vania

114. I'm skin

115. A balloon

116. A lock

117. A snowman

118. The ground is not wet

119. A riddle

120. A centipede flipped over

121. It becomes a little boulder

122. I am curiosity

123. Penguins only live in Antarctica

124. A bat

125. The answer is Frank. The mother named the kids with the first two letters of the days of the week. Monday is Marco, Tuesday is Tucker, Wednesday is Webster, Thursday is Thomas and Friday is Frank.

126. Island

127. Gone

128. I'll meet you at the corner

129. An echo

130. Your word

131. With a sea saw

132. Dancer

133. In a dictionary

134. An artichoke

135. Your own name, it's your mom, your part of the 4 children

136. grape

137. Your temper

138. A rubber band

139. There were four pears (2 pairs) on the tree. The first man took a pair (2 pears) and the second only took one pear leaving one pear on the tree.

140. Add a "g" and your Gone

141. 7, you took 7 peaches away with you. Duhhhhh

142. Because it said "concentrate"

143. What. It's pronounced differently; all of the others rhyme

144. It saw the salad dressing

145. The nose

146. A palm tree

147. Forth, is incorrectly spelled. It should be Fourth.

148. A tennis ball

149. A golf ball

150. An anchor

151. A baseball team

152. A horse

153. 1. kylie 2. Elizabeth 3. joe 4. Chris 5. john 6. Rylie 7. Kate

154. You can't dig 1/2 a hole because once you begin to dig it is an hole

155. An icicle

156. Tell it a scary story

157. Your heart

158. A matchstick

159. 17 dogs because 17-1=16-4=12-12=0+3=3-1=2

160. Because he was listening to sole music

161. Sea urchins

162. Shape the 3 matches into a Roman numeral four

163. Canary Islands

164. A comb

165. Thunderware

166. Hungary

167. X-Ray

168. A mirror

169. Bring a chair back with you

170. It overswept

171. Because of all the wrapping

172. A mongoose

173. A fence

174. A kitten

175. A sandwich

176. Sarah, Tommy, Max, Timmy, and then Sally

177. Because the students are bright

178. Tomatoes

179. Meat

180. The third. Lions that haven't eaten in three years are dead.

181. Ten Cows. We can call the pigs cows, but it doesn't make them cows.

182. Because he wants to go to High school

183. 12 of them: January 2nd, February 2nd, March 2nd, April 2nd, May 2nd, June 2nd, July 2nd, August 2nd, September 2nd, October 2nd, November 2nd, December 2nd

184. He wanted to find his friend, Pooh!

185. A watermelon

186. Ten-ish

187. The car door

188. They all do

189. In bite-size pieces

190. Darkness

191. Carpet

192. Because seven ate nine

193. A stick

194. Ghoulash

195. Edam

196. With a ruler

197. A splinter

198. A watch dog

199. A staircase

200. Spoiled milk

IMPOSSIBLE RIDDLES

201. Because they have two left feet

202. A reflection

203. The future

204. There aren't any, it's a one-story house

205. A promise

206. He was born on February 29

207. A bank

208. Yarn

209. Its lid

210. Potato

211. A cold

212. A stamp

213. A coin

214. The library

215. A coat of paint

216. Nine

217. One, two and three

218. None. He has three sisters

219. They are a grandfather, father and son

220. December 31; today is January 1.

221. Three

222. Three: A blonde, a brunette and a redhead

223. Four sisters and three brothers

224. Dozens

225. The letter 'O'

226. The letter 'R'

227. NOON

228. The word 'not'

229. Chicago

230. Few

231. Stone

232. Queue

233. Isle (add "a" to make "aisle")

234. Heroine

235. The river was frozen

236. Light

237. A key

238. Money

239. Day and night

240. Fire

241. A coffin

242. The man's son

243. A stapler

244. Because when you find it, you stop looking

245. Friday was the name of his horse

246. He only sleeps at night

247. Yesterday, today, and tomorrow

248. A yardstick

249. Your brain

250. Stars

251. 3

252. Trouble

253. The alphabet

254. A bottle

255. 5 cents

256. An earthworm

257. Corn on the cob

258. A book

259. You can see right through them

260. The spare tyre

261. A blueberry

262. It was full

263. A mushroom

264. An old-timer

265. A carpet

266. In the riverbank

267. She will let it go

268. Washington D.C.

269. The word is starting! starting, staring, string, sting, sing, sin, in, I. Cool, huh?

270. A Penny

271. An apple a day keeps the doctor away

272. The living room

273. What stairs? You live in a one-story house

274. Just one word

275. There are nine Mustards in the family. Since each daughter shares the same brother, there are six girls, one boy and Mr. and Mrs. Mustard.

276. A die (dice)

277. The woman was a photographer. She shot a picture of her husband, developed it, and hung it up to dry

278. Because it has Greece at the bottom

279. Your finger

280. There was the father, his son, and his son's son. This equals 2 fathers and 2 sons for a total of 3

281. Pencil lead

282. Monkey see monkey do

283. A pearl

284. Your identity

285. A vacuum cleaner

286. I am time

287. A windmill

288. Sleep

289. A preacher

290. An anchor

291. Opportunity

292. Your tongue

293. Earrings

294. A rocking chair

295. Impossibility

296. The two men were partners playing doubles

297. To keep its 'nuts' dry

298. You will hang me

299. I C U

300. A wedding ring

Printed in Great Britain
by Amazon